Vivien Romhoffer

Macrame

– Christmas Deco Special Edition

Table of Contents

Preface

Advent, advent, a candle burns – whenever we hear this line of a famous Christmas poem, we know that we're right in the middle of the festive period.

Advent – but what's behind this short and inconspicuous word? Advent is the time of arriving, of anticipating joyfully something really big. The festive period before Christmas offers us time to pause, enjoy, and breathe. However, if we look back on the last years and the reality it brought, we soon realize that the festive days mean a lot of stress.

Buying Christmas presents, organizing Christmas parties, decorating the house or apartment festively, taking care of the Christmas dinner, scheduling the Christmas holidays and wondering how family meetings could best be planned. Who is supposed to attend this year's Christmas meeting? Will your small apartment be spacious enough for all these people? Oh, well, and there was something else – a Christmas tree will have to be bought. But in all of that Christmas business don't we miss something else, that is time to relax, rest, peace and happiness?

We've got the solution how you can find this time to relax, get rest, peace and be happy. Plus, we've got the solution how to get around that stressful subject of buying "Christmas presents". Macrame!

How can you do that? You don't know what Macrame is? Well, in that case, you should continue reading this book: Macrame is the art of making knots. By tying together many different knots, you can create wonderful projects. All you need is the right yarn, a pair of scissors, a comb and, depending on the nature of your Macrame project, a few other items.

In the following chapters you will be given instructions on creating several Macrame Christmas projects. You may use these pieces of art as items of decoration or as Christmas presents. Are you curious? And do you wish to get down to work right away? Off we go! Take a look at the projects I'm presenting here, get yourself the right yarn and start making knots. You shall see that many projects are much easier than they might appear to you.

Hush – insider tip for you! If you love Macrame, you should in any case read our other books on the same subject, in which you find many ideas for decoration which you can use throughout the whole year.

Chapter 1
The Most Important Knots

Before you start off with your first knotting projects, you should make yourself acquainted with the most important basics. Without these basics, you will become desperate fairly soon, and your project might become either bothersome or turn out to be a failure in the end.

These basics include that you know about the range of knots you can make. Here we go:

The Overhand Knot

Take the cord, make a wrap, and bring the top end through the loop. Then pull both ends to tighten the knot.

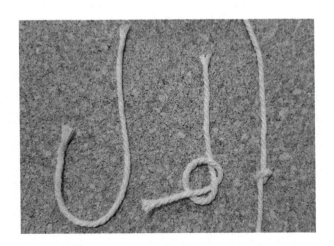

The Wave Knot

You need a total of two cords, preferably in different colours. I, for example, choose the colours yellow and red. Take the red cord and bring it over and under the yellow cord. Then, criss-cross both cords so that you obtain two loops. After that, bring the end of each cord through the loops. Both ends can now be tightened.

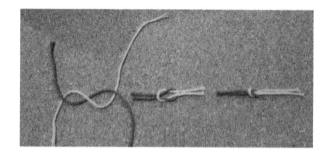

The Loop Knot

You need several cords. Double the working cord. Then wrap the bottom end around the filling cord as many times as possible. Pass the wrapping cord through the loop and pull up the top end of the wrapping cord, so the know will disappear under the wrap. Then cut off both ends of the wrap.

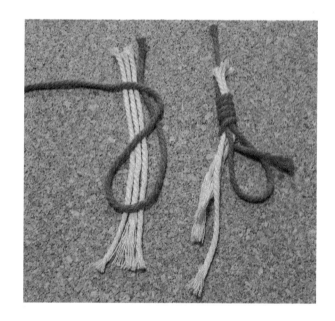

The Figure Eight Knot

Place a cord on the table. Pass its lower end over itself to form the figure eight. Continue over and under the cord, so it can be passed through the lower belly of the eight. Then tighten the knot at both ends.

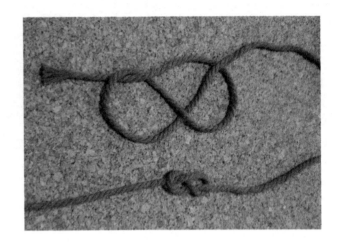

The Carrick Bend Left

Place four cords next to each other. Take the outermost cord on the left and place it over the other cords in such a manner as to form an L. Then move the outermost cord on the right over the L-shaped cord, under the middle cords and, finally, through the loop. Repeat everything the other way round. The right carrick bend is knotted the same way, however, you start off on the right side.

The Anchor Knot

Place the working cord over and under the middle cords. Then feed the working cord into the loop and tighten the knot. Repeat everything and tighten the knot.

Right Anchor Knot:

Left Anchor Knot:

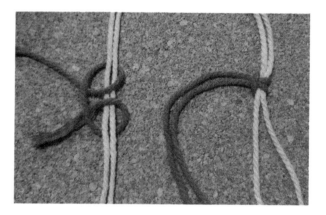

The Clove Hitch

Make sure that the working cord is longer than the other cords. Place the working cord over the other cords in such as manner as to form an L. This cord is never pulled tight, but only hold fast. Now, take the first cord next to the working cord and move it under and over the working cord and, finally, through the loop. This procedure is always repeated to make sure the knot is tight enough. To make the Left Clove Hitch you start off on the left side, the Right Clove Hitch on the right side.

Right Clove Hitch:

Left Clove Hitch:

Chapter 2
Ring With Tree

What would Christmas be without a Christmas tree? However, if you are not in the mood to get yourself a tree, which will lose its needles anyway, or if it makes no sense for you to buy one because you haven't got enough space in your flat, things can turn out to be bothersome and annoying. I've got the solution for you! How about a self-made Macrame Christmas tree for hanging up? If you like, you may combine several trees in one. The following instructions will show you how to create your Christmas tree in a ring. I wish you the best of success for your project!

Materials

- Macrame yarn in the colours of your choice
- Metal ring
- Wooden stick
- Pair of scissors
- Comb
- Small decorative items if you wish
  (for example stars)

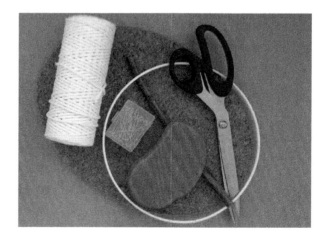

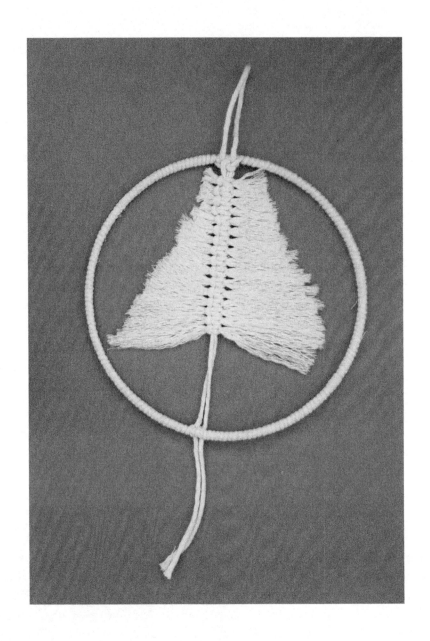

1

Cut a cord to measure. This one can be a bit longer for making the pendant and fixing the bottom ends.

2

Double your cord and bring the loop to your ring in such a manner as to be used as a pendant later in the process. Take one of the two ends and wrap it around the ring once, producing a loop. Then pass the loose end through the loop. Repeat everything and pull your anchor knot tight.

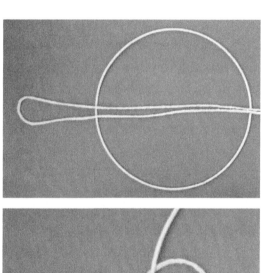

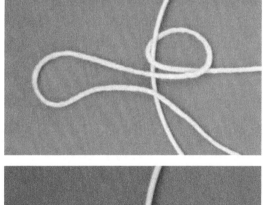

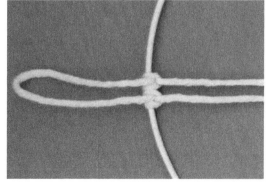

3

Take the other end and do the same as before. Having made both anchor knot and fixed the cord to the ring, you repeat everything at the bottom end of the ring so that the two cords are stretching tight in the middle.

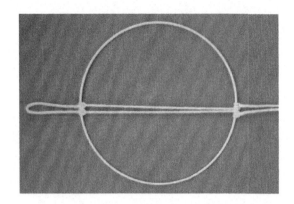

4

Take your Macrame yarn and wrap it around the ring. Or you can cut to measure two cords with a minimum length of 2 m and tie the wave knot around the ring. Actually, it's a half carrick knot you're having, and which must be passed around the ring. Make the left cord into an L and place it over the ring and the middle cords. Then take the right cord and place it over the L-shaped cord, pull it down and move it up through the loop of the L-shaped cord. Tighten everything. Then make more half knots, and soon you will understand the reason for the name of the knot: Your strand is beginning to form a wave.

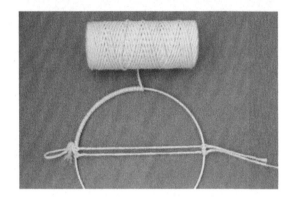

5

When your ring is completely covered with cords, you cut to measure some shorter cords with a length of about 20 cm. These cords, whose length depends on the actual size of your project, are used for knotting the tree itself.

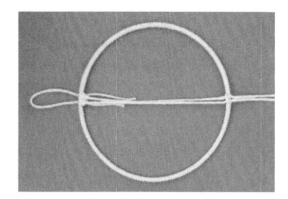

6

That's how you create your tree: Double one cord and bring it under the trunk of the tree. Take another cord, double it, and pass its loose ends through the loop of the first cord. Now, the loop of the second cord is on the loose ends of the first cord. Take the loose ends and pass them through the loop. Then pull everything tight.

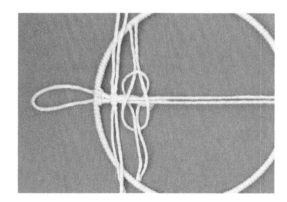

7

Proceed with step 6 until your tree has reached the size of your choice. Then comb the cords you inserted as thoroughly as possible.

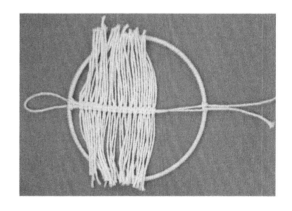

8

In order to cut your tree to measure, I suggest drawing a triangle on a piece of cardboard cut it out and place your cords where they're supposed to be. You can cut your tree to measure along its edges.

9

If you like a tree that's more stable than that, take hairspray and apply it several times. Then let it dry.

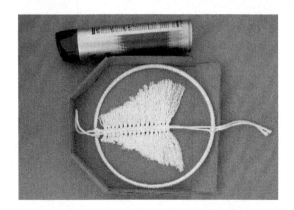

10

Your first Christmas tree has been finished. All that needs to be done now is tie the wooden stick to a cord on both sides. Everything will look beautiful even without such a stick. Finally, you may decorate the tree(s) you made with items like stars or other things.

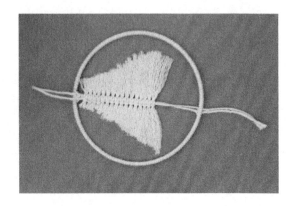

Chapter 3
Imp

Like Christmas trees, even diligent Christmas imps take part in the festivity of love. Well, they are there to help Santa Claus package the presents for all kids of the world. Following these easy instructions, you can create one or even more of these imps.

Materials

- Macrame yarn in the colours of your choice.
- White Macrame yarn
- Wooden pearl
- Pair of scissors
- Comb
- Empty toilet paper roll
- Hot glue or superglue

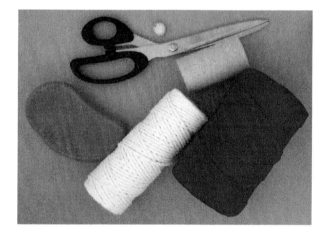

1

Cut to measure a minimum total of 30 cords with a length of 30 cm. Depending on the size of your empty toilet paper roll, you may need more or less cords.

2

Take the roll and cut off a ring-shaped piece of it, which should at least be having the width of your fingertip.

3

Take a cord with a length of 30 cm, double it and bring the loop through the toilet paper ring. Pass the loose ends through the loop and do the same with the other cords.

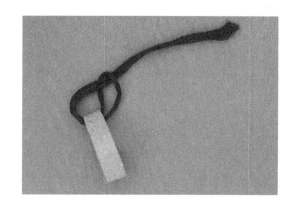

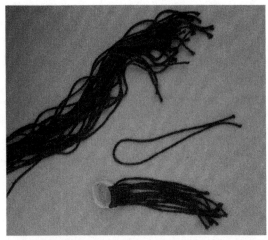

4

You may try out the following now: Bring the
cords through the roll and tie them together
at the top bottom end as to produce a hat.
You may alternatively tie the cords without
bringing them through the loop. Just do as
you like.

5

Cut to measure the cords you need for your bobble and wrap another cord around it which you will later use to hang up your project. The imps you made can be hung up on a tree or attached to a present.

6

Put the hat aside. Then take the white yarn and wrap it around your hand several times. It's up to you how thick the beard of the imp is going to be.

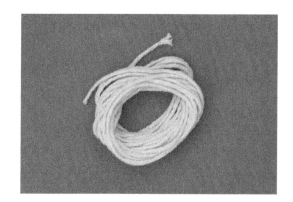

7

Then take the bundle of cords off again, make a cut into the end of the toilet paper roll and put the bundle on the table. Always proceed very carefully. Cut off a piece of the cord, take your wooden pearl and thread it onto the cord.

8

Put the cord with the pearl on your bundle of cords, pass the loose ends from the bottom through the bundle so that they're protruding on both sides. Tie them together as fast as possible. Then cut open the bottom end and comb the cords well, thus creating hair and beard.

9

Take the hot glue. Give a drop of it on the inner ring of your hat (top and bottom), place the bundle of cords that form the beard of your imp inside and attach the hat as tightly as possible. Be careful not to burn yourself.

10

Finally, cut open the bottom end of the beard and comb the cords. You're done! This is your imp!

Chapter 4
Angel In Picture Frame

"Angels, we have heard on high." That's one of the most beautiful and well-known Christmas carols. What about a really unique Macrame angel set in a picture frame? Take a look at the following instructions, and you will realize that you can come close to fulfilling your wish with a few steps only.

Materials

- Macrame yarn in the colours of your choice
- Picture frame
- Wooden ball
- Paper
- Pair of scissors
- Comb

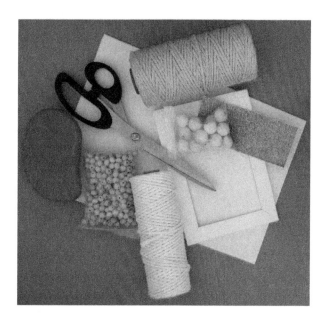

Step-by-Step Instructions

1

Take a picture frame, take out the glass and glue white paper on the back of the frame.

2

Then draw the wings of your angel on a sheet of paper, cut everything out and take hot glue to fix the wings on the white background.

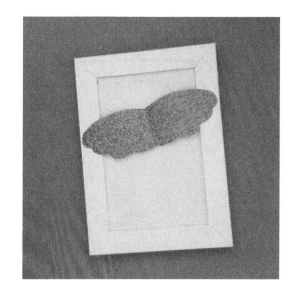

3

Cut to measure about 15 cords of your choice that you need for your angel's dress. Double the cords and tie them together in the middle by means of another cord.

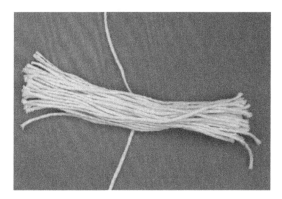

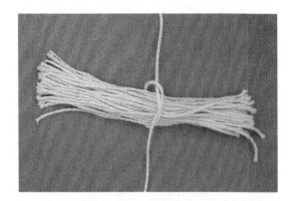

4

Comb the cords on both sides and put the bundle together.

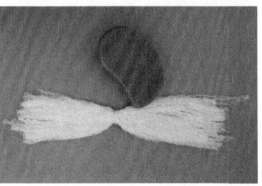

5

Cut to measure to further cords. One of them must be placed between your other cords, that is in such a manner as to use it for the arms of your angel later on in the process. Advice: Take a few drops of hot glue to fix it. Then cut to measure one more cord, pass it through the ball and pull one of its ends through the torso. Tie both ends together and tighten everything well.

6

Then take the second cord to tie the bundle together at the bottom part of your project, thus creating a torso and a dress. Cut to measure the ends of the angel's dress as beautifully as possible.

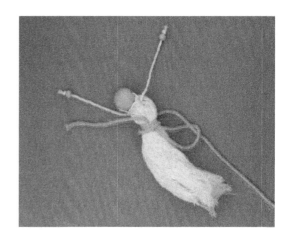

7

Take the other colour for your angel's hair and wrap the cord around your hand as you did it before. Pull the bundle of cords off your hand again and put it on the table. Proceed carefully.

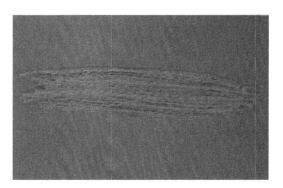

8

Comb the cords well. Then glue the bundle to your ball and comb the hair into shape. If need be, you may also cut the ends to measure.

9

Your angel in the picture frame is almost finished now. Take hot glue and fix the angel to the white paper, respectively to the wings you previously fixed. You may also glue to it a paper star or other small decorative items, thus creating the impression your angel is holding them fast.

Chapter 5
Star Money

The festive period is also the right time for fairy tales. Do you know the tale of star money? Imagine, by using Macrame you can also design your own decoration. You want to know how it works? Then take a closer look at the following instructions.

Materials

- Macrame yarn in the colours of your choice
- Picture frame
- Wooden ball
- Decorative star items
- Pair of scissors
- Comb

1

First, take the glass out of the picture frame. Then take your paper and draw a square on it, which you glue on the black of your frame. As a template, you should use the glass plate. As a background, you may take paper in a colour of your choice.

2

Take your stars and decide for yourself how many of them you want to use. Glue them to the picture frame as you wish. I, for myself, picked the upper corner on the left for positioning these decorative items.

3

Cut to measure about 15 cords in a colour of your choice to be used later for your girl's dress. Double them and make them into a bundle by means of another cord.

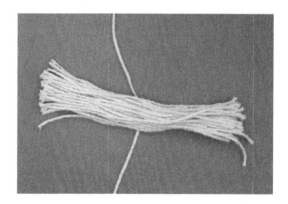

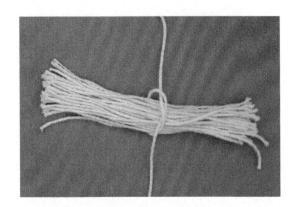

4

Comb out the cords to both sides. Then re-assemble your bundle.

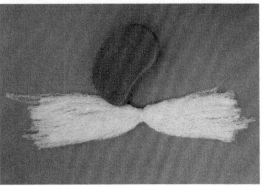

5

Cut to measure, two further cords. One of them is placed between your cords, that is in such a manner as to be used later for your girl's arms. Advice: Fix that cord with a drop of hot glue. Then cut to measure one more cord, pass it through the ball and pull one of the ends through the torso. Tie both ends together at the top end of the ball.

6

Then take the second cord and tie the bottom bundle together, thus producing a torso and a dress. Cut the ends of the dress carefully into shape.

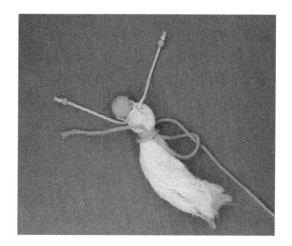

7

Take cords with another colour for your girl's hair. Wrap the cord around your hand like you did it when making your imp. Then pull the bundle from your hand again and place it on the table. Proceed with care.

8

Cut off another cord and pass it through the loop. Then tie both ends together while tightening everything well.

9

Comb the cords well. Glue the bundle of cords to the ball and comb the hair into shape. If need be, you may cut to measure the ends of the cords.

10

You're almost done! Take some hot glue and fix the shape of the girl to the white paper. The picture frame can now be placed somewhere or hung up on the wall.

Chapter 6
Candy Cane

Sweets and candies belong to the festive Christmas period like lights, candles and presents. People who wish to decorate their Christmas tree or their apartment with Macrame projects, shouldn't miss out on the following instructions for knotting a candy cane. It can be created very easily using different colours or the traditional red-and-white combination.

Materials

- Red Macrame yarn
- White Macrame yarn
- Wire
- Pair of scissors
- Cork plate
- Pin

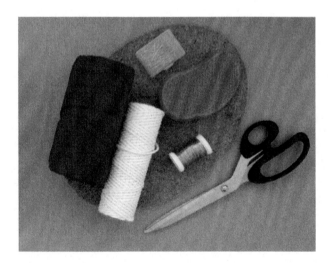

Step-by-Step Instructions

1

Cut to measure a red cord with the length of
at least 100 cm. Do the same with your white
yarn.

2

Criss-cross both cords over each other. Take
a pin to fix the middle-section where both
cords are crossing to your cork plate. This
adds more stability to your project.

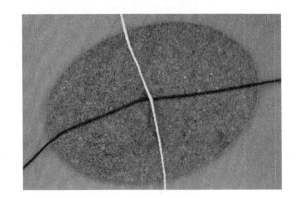

3

Proceed as follows: Place the bottom cord
over the cord next to it on the left, thus producing a big loop. Then take the left cord and
place it in the same manner over the top
cord.

4

Place the top cord over the cord on the right.
Then this cord is brought through the loop of
the bottom cord, which was placed over the
cord on the left.

5

Pull at the ends of your four cords until they join in the middle-section and filling the pin.

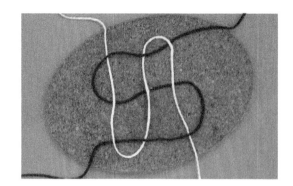

6

Proceed with steps 3 to 5 in exactly the same manner and having completed three rounds insert some wire which should have a length of about 5 cm. This wire is later used to get your cane into shape.

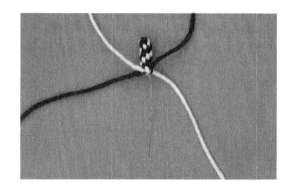

7

Continue knotting until your candy cane has reached the size you wish.

8

Cut off a long cord in order to seal the end of your cane with a wrap knot. Proceed as follows: Part of one end of the cord should be on the cane. Take the other one to make it into a loop and wrap it around your four cords. Pull the bottom end through the loop. Then take both ends of your wrapping cord and pull at its bottom end until the knot slips under the wrap. Your wrap knot is done!

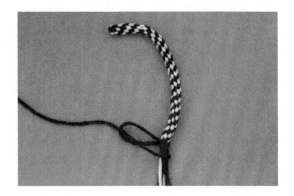

9

Cut your cords to measure, as you please, and comb them well. Get your candy cane into shape by bending the spot where you inserted the wire. Then cut off another cord, tie it to the bend of your candy cane, so you can hang it up on the tree.

Chapter 7
Knotting Made Easy

People who have tried out more than one Macrame project know for sure that knotting can be rather difficult sometimes. I'd like to take this opportunity to give you some advice for making knotting easier for you.

❖ Use the clipboards

Actually, some projects need to be stabilized, so they can't slip off while you're at work. The best choice for this purpose is a clipboard, which means that you can fix the top part of your project to the board while working with the bottom part of it. Everything remains stable and in place.

❖ Adhesive tape

If you don't have a clipboard at your disposal, you may take a thick adhesive tape and fix your Macrame project to a table, thereby giving it the stability, it needs.

❖ Rolling clothes rail

Some Macrame projects are really complex. In order to keep them stable and have enough space for work, it's recommendable to fix them to a rolling clothes rail. These rails can be adjusted in height, and you can work while standing or being seated.

❖ Hooks, chair backs & Co.

If you don't want to buy yourself one of these moveable rails for your projects, you can also take simple hooks, stainless steel S-shaped hooks for example. You can fix them very easily to doors or chairs, and you may also hang up a knotting rail on them. Or you may have chairs, whose backs have decorative holes through which such a rail may be passed.

❖ Rolling up long cords

Bigger projects need more amount of yarn. So, in such a case your cords are long, and you may end up having entangled cords. You can prevent that from happening by rolling up your cords that far as to produce small "balls" hanging down from them. You may roll them up again and again, should your working cord have become too short.

Chapter 8
Star

It was a star that showed the Three Magi the way to the cradle of Jesus. It's a must-have for Christmas! By using Macrame, you can create wonderful decorative stars. If you love stars and use them as decorative elements during the festive period, you will definitely like to follow these instructions.

Materials

- Yellow Macrame yarn
- Pin
- Cork plate
- Pair of scissors
- Wooden ring
- Comb

1

Cut to measure a total of 40 cords with a length of 80 cm, which you fix to the ring by means of an anchor knot.

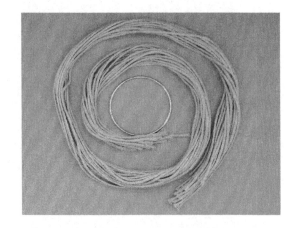

2

Take a cord and double it. Then pass the loop under the ring and feed the loose ends into it.

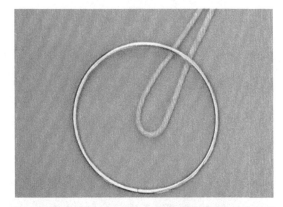

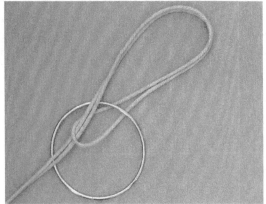

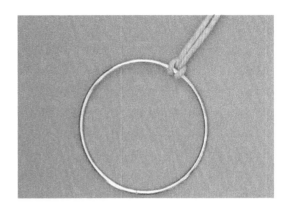

3

Do the same with the other cords. Then divide the number of your cords into five groups with eight cords.

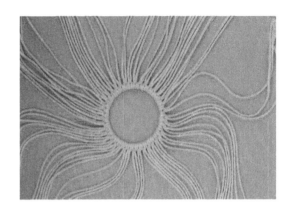

4

Take the four cords next to each other and make them into two carrick bends. Place three cords in the middle. Take the left cord and place it L-shaped over the middle cords. The right cord is placed over the L and then passed under the middle cords and through the L-loop. Pull everything tight and repeat these steps with the right side to finish your carrick bend. After that, you make three more carrick bends.

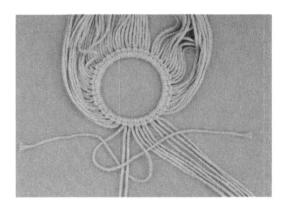

5

Put two cords aside on each side. Then tie an offset row of three carrick bends. When finished, put two cords aside on each side and start the next offset row of carrick bends. Repeat it one more time in order to finish your carrick bend. Do the same with the other four cord groups to finally get five teeth of carrick bends.

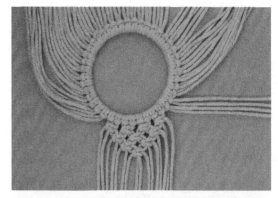

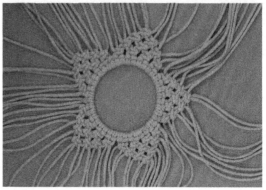

6

Cut off the protruding yarn or tie clove hitches around the teeth. To make a clove hitch, proceed as follows: Take the outmost cord on the left of one of the teeth and place it as your working cord over the other cords. Then wrap the cord next to it around the working cord twice. Repeat this with the next cords until you've come to the end of a tooth. Then repeat these steps on the right side of the tooth. Having reached the end of the tooth, you can tie both working cords together. Do the same with the other teeth of your project.

If you have decided to make your cords into a clove hitch, proceed as I did: Having cut off the protruding yarn, you comb the cords carefully. Fix the fringes by applying hairspray and cut them to measure, if need be.

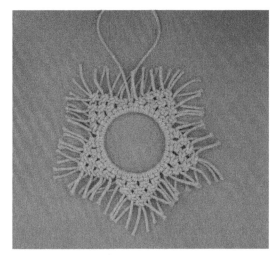

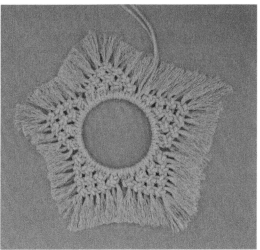

Chapter 8
Hanging Advent Wreath

"Advent, advent, a little light is burning." An advent wreath that can be put on the table can be found in nearly every home during the festive period. What about surprising your guests with a hanging advent wreath? Then take a look at the following instructions, and you will realize that it's not difficult at all to create such wreath yourself.

Materials

- Four glasses
- A large metal ring
- Red Macrame yarn
- Thin white and red yarn

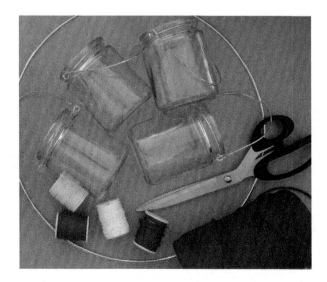

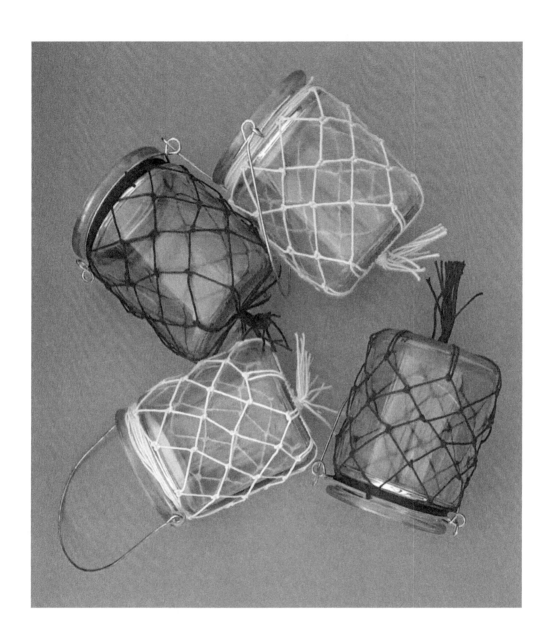

1

Cut to measure six cords with a length of your choice. Put three of them aside. Take the first three of them and make them into a loop at the bottom end in order to fix it to your ring with an anchor knot. Important: For only a small part of your project the cords should be doubled, that means, one part of the cord is long, while the other part is kept short. The shorter part will later be threaded into the strand.

2

Having fixed your cords, you start braiding. Make sure that the shorter cords are always kept together by one longer cord. It's easier for you to integrate them into the strand so that they won't be seen anymore.

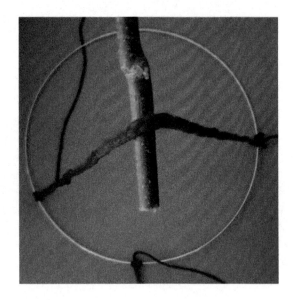

3

If your braiding strand has the right length, you tie the cords to the other side with a simple anchor knot. Make sure to hold fast your cords on ring. Take the first of them and wrap it around the ring, thus producing a loop through which you pull the loose end of the cord. Tighten everything well and repeat this step so that the cord will be tightly fixed to the ring.

4

Repeat this procedure with the other cords. Now you've got a hanger for your wreath. But since it is no stable enough, take the other three cords and repeat steps 1 to 4 with them. In the end, your braiding strands should be placed in such a manner as to form a cross. If you miscalculated the length, you could cut to measure four cords with a length of your choice and make them into a row of carrick bends. Pass this row under the cross and connect it to form a hook by tying the loose ends together by means of a wrap knot.

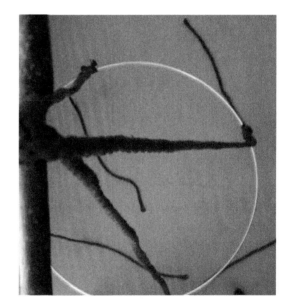

5

Cut to measure as many cords you like to use for every glass. When doubled, they should at least be twice as long as the glass itself.

6

Cover the edges of your glasses with yarn, which you need to attach the cords you cut to measure.

7

Take a glass and attach your cords to it. Double them and pass the loop under the cords. Move the loose ends through the loop and pull them tight.

8

If all cords have been knotted around the glass, take one cord from two anchor knots that are next to each other. Then tie them together by making a simple shoe knot. Repeat everything, since one knot alone wouldn't add the stability, you need.

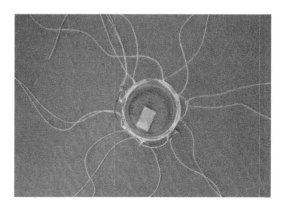

9

Proceed with your project so that you can create a first knot ring. For the second knot ring you take again two cords from two anchor knots that are next to each other and proceed as before.

10

Repeat these steps until you come to the bottom of your glass. Cut to measure a longer cord which you need for the next step.

11

Take all cords together, twist them in a little and make the prepared cords into a wrap knot around the other cords. Pull everything tight, so the pattern of the glass becomes clearly visible.

12

Cut the fringes on the bottom of the glass to a length you like most. Take the other three cords and proceed as before.

13

Now you may make further braiding
strands to attach your glasses to the ring.

Advice:

You may miss in here the descriptions on how to create a Christmas style ring. That's my intention because it's up to you to use your own creativity and make your own designs. These instructions are meant to be of help to you to create a kind of basic structure for your Macrame advent wreath.

Chapter 10
Snowflake

"Little snowflake, little white skirt, when will you be snowing?"

For us, snow belongs to Christmas. Sometimes, however, it's coming quite late in the season, or it won't be snowing at all. Using these easy instructions, you can get yourself a lot of snow into your home, if you wish. And the advantage is that it's not going to be cold.

Materials

- White Macrame yarn
- Pair of scissors
- Cork plate
- Pins
- Comb
- Wooden ring

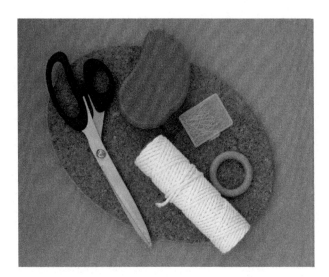

1

Cut a total of 21 cords with a length of about 50 cm to measure. Fix them to your ring with an anchor knot which purpose you double the single cords. Pass the loop under the ring and move the loose ends through it. Proceed like that with all the other cords. Pick one of your cords to use as a hanger and tie the loose ends together.

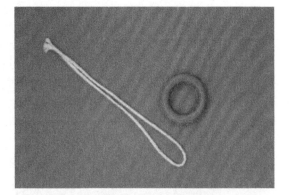

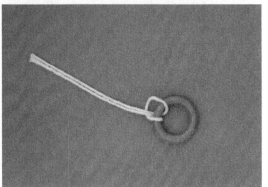

2

Take a pin and fix the hanger to a cork plate, so you have enough stability for knotting.

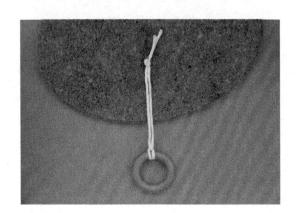

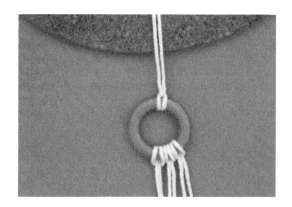

3

Take four cords that are next to each other and make them into four carrick knots. Place two cords in the middle. Then take the left cord and place it L-shaped over the middle cords. Pass the right cord over the L and under the middle cords, then through the L-loop. Pull everything tight and repeat these steps on the right side to complete your carrick knot. After that, you make three further carrick bends.

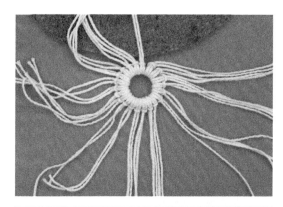

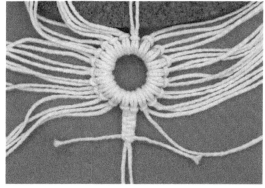

4

Proceed with making carrick bends with all your cords until you've got ten strands of them.

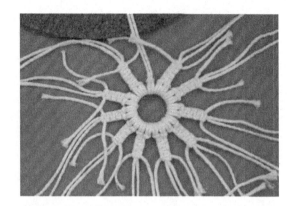

5

Take two cords from two strands with carrick bends and make them into one to two carrick bends.

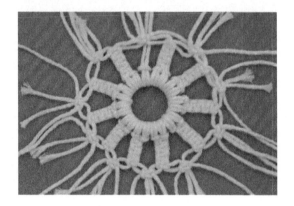

6

Proceed with step 5 until you have tied together all strands.

7

Comb the ends of the cords and cut them as fringes and to a length of your choice. If need be, you may apply hairspray to fix the fringes.

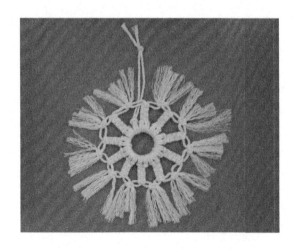

Chapter 11
Santa Claus

In most families, it's customary that Santa Claus is bringing the Christmas presents. Considering that, I think there is also need for decoration. Following these instructions, you can magically create wonderful decorative items for Christmas tree and for your windows.

Materials

- Red Macrame yarn
- White Macrame yarn
- Pair of scissors
- Needle
- Sewing yarn, preferably in red
- Wooden pearl
- Comb

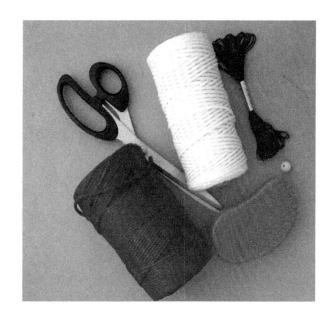

1

Cut to measure two cords with a length of 450 cm. Double both cords. Then you move the two loops into each other, yet without making them into a knot. Take the outermost cord on the left and place it L-shaped over the two inner cords. Take the outermost cord on the right, place it over the L-shaped cord and pass it under the cords and through the L-loop. Pull everything tight and repeat these steps from the right side. Make further carrick bends until the strand is long enough for your purposes.

2

Then tie the two cords on the left with each other at the end of the strand. Do the same with the two cords on the right. Cut off the protruding yarn.

3

Place your strand in such a manner as to produce a pyramidal shape. Press everything in place to make sure it's stable. Take a needle and sewing yarn in order to sew the individual steps of the pyramid to each other.

4

Thread another cord with both its ends onto the needle and pass them through the top section of the hat so that one loop remains up there. Before you pass your needle further through the loop, you may make a knot above the top to prevent it from being pulled right through it.

5

Take the pearls and thread in onto one of your doubled cords. Tie it to the bottom part of the pearl, so it can be tight-fitting.

6

Take your white yarn and cut to measure a number of short cords. Double them, take a crochet needle or something else to move them through the loops at the bottom of your hat.

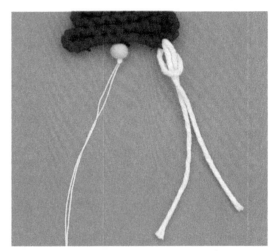

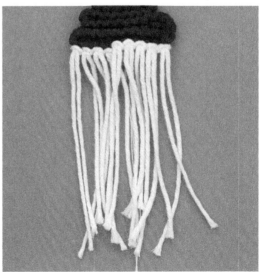

7

Comb out the white cords to create a beautiful beard for your Santa. Fix it with hairspray and cut it into final shape.

Chapter 12
Angel

"Angels we have heard on high" is one of the most celebrated Christmas carols about angels. If you like angels, too, the following instructions will be truly a must for you. Following them, you can create yourself a unique angel which you may also take as a wonderful Christmas present.

Materials

- Ring
- White Macrame yarn
- Pair of scissors
- Comb
- Wooden pearls
- Yellow yarn
- Ball

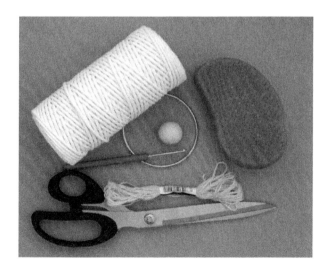

1

Cut to measure a total of 28 cords with a length of 35 cm. Then cut to measure further six cords with a length of 30 cm. Furthermore, you need one cord with a length of 50 cm for fixing the ball.

2

Double the long cord and pass the loop through the ring. Then bring both loose ends through the loop to pull the cord tight.

3

Bring the ball onto both cords. If it's a bit difficult, you may take a crochet needle. Move the ball up to the top edge of the ring. Take the right cord, move it over the ring and through the loop. Repeat these steps one more time with the left cord.

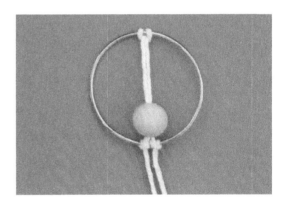

4

Take your cords with a length of 35 cm and fix them to your ring with anchor knot. There should be 14 cords on each side.

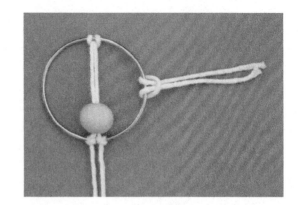

5

Comb all cords to create the wings of the angel. You may either comb them upward or downwards, as you like.

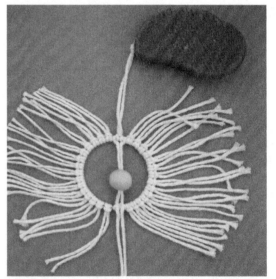

6

To add stability to your project, you may apply some hairspray to the angel.

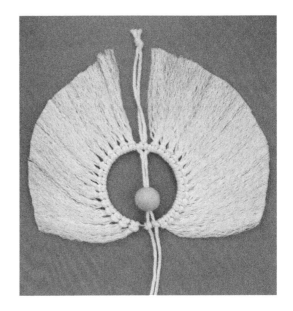

7

Put the six cords with the same length on your table and comb them well. After that, you fold the "carpet" you've got now in the middle. But only once. Then move it under the ball through the ring.

8

Cut to measure two more cords, one of which may be even a bit shorter. Then fix a wooden pearl to the end of both cords. The cords must then be put into the angel's body.

9

Take appropriately thin yarn and place the cord on the bundle of combed cords, that is in such manner as to make the top end become clearly visible and to enable you to make a loop at the bottom. Wrap it around the bundle of combed cords, move the end of the thin cord through the loop and pull at the top end in order to hide the knot under the wrap. Then cut off protruding yarn.

10

Cut off a cord with a length of 20 cm and fix it above your ball with an anchor knot, so you can hang up your angel later. Moreover, your angel needs some hair, for which purpose you take thin yarn in the colour of your choice and repeat step 7. The thickness of the angel's hair is up to you. Glue the ball, that makes the angel's head, to the body and then the hair to the top end of the ball. That's your finished angel!

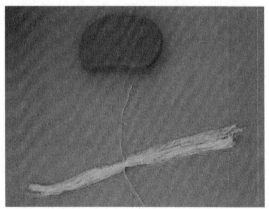

Chapter 13
Garland With Light And Pendant

Not only Mardi Gras knows garlands. With a little light and the right colours, you may create wonderful Christmas garlands. Take a look at the following instructions, and you will realize how easy it is to tie a garland.

Materials

- Red Macrame yarn
- White Macrame yarn
- Wooden pearls
- Pair of scissors
- Comb
- Light chain

1

Cut the measure one cord with a length of your choice and make a loop at its one end and then thread a wooden pearl onto it.

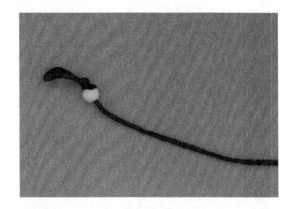

2

Cut to measure a total of six red cords with a length of 60 cm. Double them and fix them to your cord with an anchor knot. For doing that you double every single cord, push the loop under the cord and bring the loose ends through the loop.

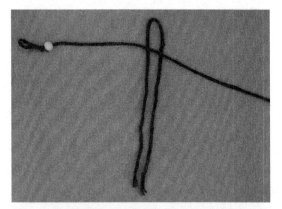

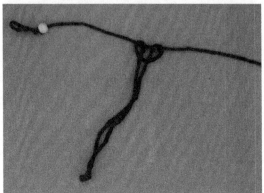

3

Having fixed all cords, you tie a row of car-rick bends. Take four cords that are next to each other. Take the outermost cord on the left and place it L-shaped over the two inner cords. Then take the outermost cord on the right, place it over the L-shaped cord, move it under the cords and through the L-loop. Pull everything tight and repeat these steps from the right.

4

Then put aside two cords on each side and tie an offset row with two carrick bends. Re-peat that one more time to finish up with a carrick bend. Cut off the protruding yarn as you like and comb it well. The whole can take the shape of a feather. In order to fix everything, you may apply hairspray.

5

Now it's time for another pearl. After that, you can tie the next feather made of carrick bends to it. Your garland is designed to have pearls and knotted feathers in turns. The length of your garland is up to you.

6

Take the light chain and move it through the garland as you please.

Chapter 14
Wall Hanging Tree With Bar

A tree mustn't necessarily be placed in a room. It can also be used as a decorative wall hanging. Take a look at the following instructions. I'm sure you will like it.

Materials

- Two wooden sticks
- Green Macrame yarn
- Light chain
- Pairs of scissors
- Comb

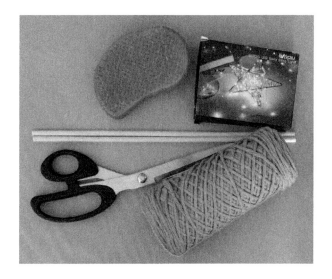

1

Cut to measure a total of 20 cords with a length of 1.50 cm.

2

Fix all cords to your first bar by making them into anchor knots. Double every single cord, move the loop under the cord and bring the loose ends through the loop.

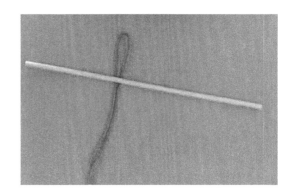

3

Divide your cords and take two cords from the left and two cords from the right side. Make them into a carrick bend, which will be the top of your tree. And it's up to you whether there is going to be some empty space between the tree and the bar. For the carrick bend, you take the outermost left cord and place it L-shaped over the two inner cords. Take the outermost cord on the right, place it over the L-cord and move it under the cords and through the loop. Tighten everything well and repeat these steps from the right.

4

Take two cords from each side so that you have a total of eight cords in front of you. Take them to make two carrick bends. Proceed like that in row no. 3. With every new row you add one more carrick bend. Proceed until you've got a triangle.

5

After that, you start knotting a second triangle under the first triangle. Start off with dividing your cords, as you did in step 3. Repeat steps 4 and 5 until you finished the second triangle.

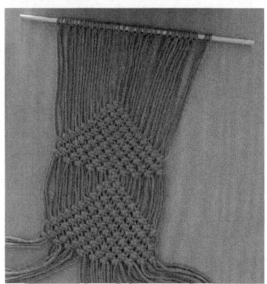

6

Take 12 cords from each side and put them aside. The remaining cords are used to tie four or more rows of offset carrick bends, which you use for the trunk of your tree.

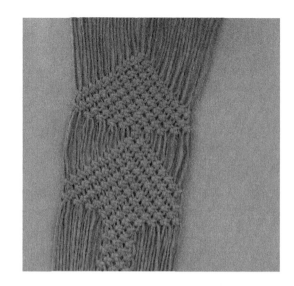

7

Now it's time to use your second wooden stick, for which you make an anchor knot. Take every single cord and proceed as follows: Start off with the cords for the trunk that give stability to your tree project. Place one cord over the stick, thus producing a loop through which you pass the loose end. Repeat everything one more time and pull the cord as tight as possible. Do the same with the other cords.

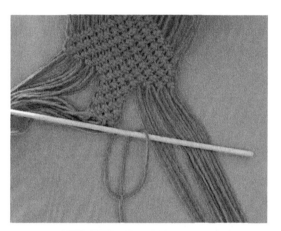

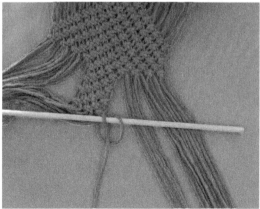

8

Now it's your decision whether you connect all cords with a wrap knot or whether you simply comb them out. For making a wrap knot, you cut off one more cord. Take all cords and hold them fast. Place the new cord in such a manner as to make sure its top end is reaching over the bar. Take the other end and make it into a loop which you're holding fast with one finger. Wrap it around the cords several times. Finally, you bring the loose end through the loop. Then pull at both ends to make the knot disappear under the wrap. Cut the ends of the cords to have equal length.

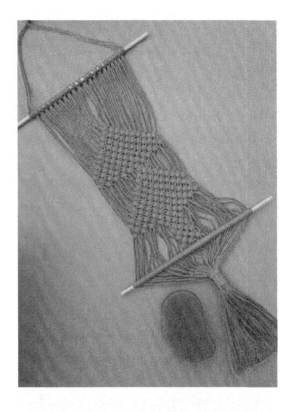

9

Move your light chain through your wall hanging as you please.

Chapter 15
Tied-In Ball

Beautiful balls belong to every Christmas tree decoration. How about creating a set of balls yourself? That would definitely be a true eye-catcher for your guests.

Materials

- Thin Macrame yarn in the colours of your choice
- Plastic Christmas balls
- Pair of scissors

1

Cut to measure ten cords with a length o7 90 cm. Additionally, you need one cord with a length of 25 cm.

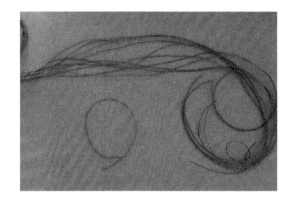

2

Make an anchor knot and use it to fix these ten cords to the one shorter cord. Then double every single cord, move the loop under the cord and feed the loose ends into the loop. In order to make everything look prettier, you proceed as follows: Take the left cord, wrap it around your main cord producing a loop. Then pull the loose end through it. Proceed like that with the right cord, too. And do the same with all of your ten cords. You will be having a beautiful and stable edge for your ball.

3

Take the garland and place it around the neck of the ball. Tie the loose ends together as best as you can. By removing the fixture of the ball and putting it into the ball, you can make the protruding yarn disappear very easily.

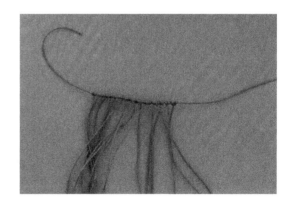

4

Now, you've got two options to tie in your ball:

- Option 1: Take all cords and tie them together with a wrap knot under the ball.

- Option 2: Take for cords that are next to each other and make them into a carrick bend. Proceed like that with all other cords until you've got a row of bends surrounding the ball.

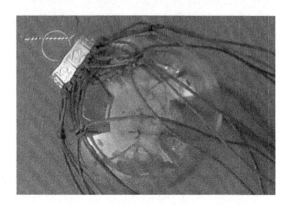

5

Take two cords from the two carrick bends next to each other and make them into another row of bends. Proceed like that until your ball is fully covered with yarn.

6

Take the protruding yarn and fix it with a wrap knot. Cut off one more cord for making your wrap knot. Take all cords in one hand and position the new cord in such a manner as to make its top end reaching over the bar. Make the other end into a loop which you're holding with a finger. Wrap it around the cords several times and, finally, pass the loose end through the loop. Pull at both ends until the knot has disappeared under the wrap. Cut the ends to have equal height.

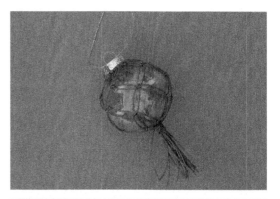

Chapter 16
Heart Angel

Angels belong to Christmas. No doubt. Their wings impress us again and again. Take a look at the following instructions for making yourself a wonderful angel you can use to decorate your walls or your window during the festive season.

Materials

- Metal heart
- White Macrame yarn
- Thin yarn in various colours of your choice
- Comb
- Pair of scissors
- Wooden balls

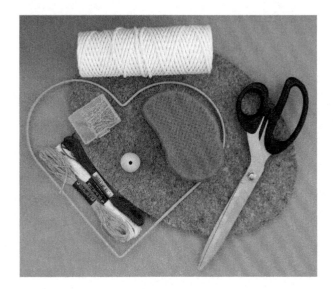

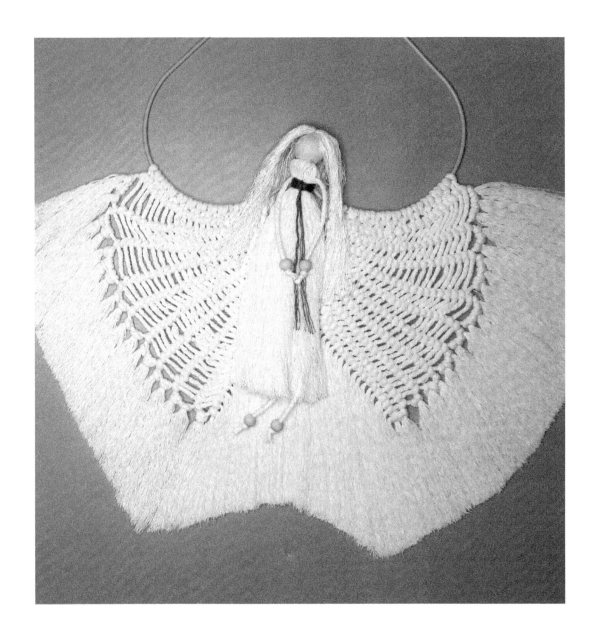

1

Cut to measure about 15 cords you take for the dress of your angel. Double them and take another cord to tie them together in the middle. Comb the cords to both sides and gather your bundle again.

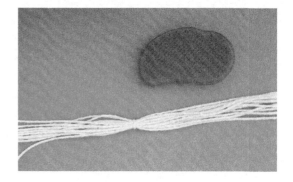

2

Cut to measure, two more cords. Place them between your cords, so you can use later them for the arms and legs of your angel. Advice: Take a few drops of hot glue to fix it. If you like, you may create the hands and legs of your angel with small wooden pearls, or you may simply tie a knot into the cord.

3

Take a cord in a colour of your choice to tie the belt you use for the dress. You need to make a wrap knot. Place the cord over the dress, that is, in such a manner as to make one end reach over it. The other end at the bottom is made into a loop and wrap it around the body of your angel. The cord shouldn't be too loose or too tight. If your belt is thick enough, pass the loose end through the loop. Then pull at the top end of the cord, so the knot can slip under the

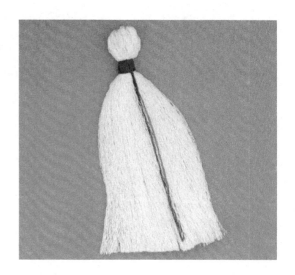

wrap. Cut the ends of your dress into
shape and comb everything, if need be.

4

Take yarn in another colour for the hair of
your angel. Wrap the cord around your
hand, as you did when making the beard of
your Christmas imp. Pull it off your hand
again and place it carefully on the table.
Comb the cords well. Glue the bundle to
the ball and comb the hair into shape. If
need be, you may cut the ends of the cords
into shape. Then, take glue and fix the ball
to the body of your angel.

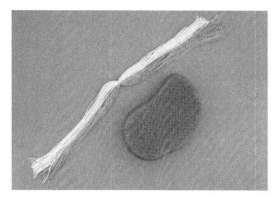

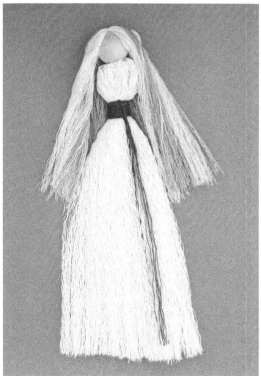

5

Put the angel aside and continue with the wings, for which purpose you need your metal heart and ten cords with a length of 230 cm and 14 cords with a length of 190 cm. Make an anchor knot and fix them to the metal heart. Double the cord and pass the loop under the metal heart. Then move the loose ends through the loop so that the cords are fixed well to the heart.

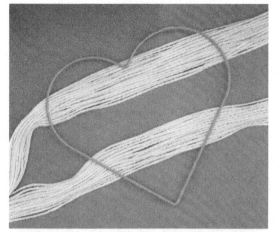

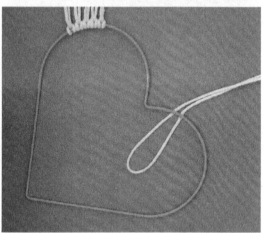

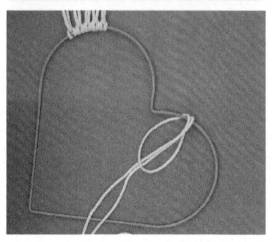

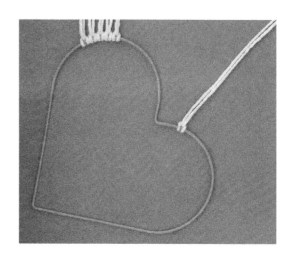

6

Start off with the longer cords. There must be five cords with a length of 230 cm inside every bow of the heart, and there have to be seven cords with a length of 190 cm outside.

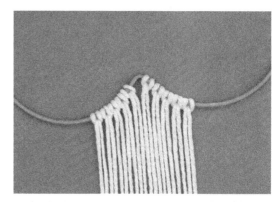

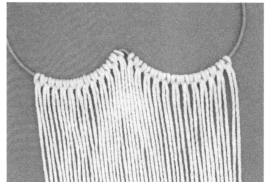

7

If that's done, you pick one side you wish to begin with. Take the first inner cord and place it over the other cords. Take the second cord and wrap a clove hitch around the main cord. To do that, you tie a loop under the main cord and pull the loose end through it. Since this one knot wouldn't be tight enough, you repeat these steps. Important: Always pull on the working cord. Never pull on the main cord. Otherwise, you won't be able to make your clove hitches. Repeat everything with all other cords until you've got your first row.

8

Now place the cord you used as main cord, at the back. Take the next cord, which is the first one to be inside, as your new main cord. Repeat step 6 and make sure that you pull the first ten cords very closely to the first row of clove hitches. Avoid a too large gap, or you can't get your wings in shape. The gap can be larger after these ten cords.

9

Repeat step 6 until you've got ten rows of carrick bends. Proceed like that with the other side to make the second wing.

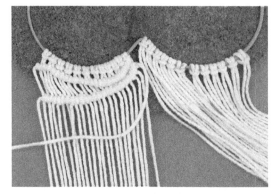

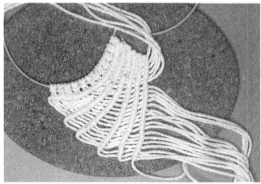

10

Cut to measure some small cords or use the remaining yarn you've got from other Macrame projects. Double them and pass the loop through the gaps in the outermost part of the wings. Move the loose ends through the loop, thus tightening the cord. Repeat everything until you've come to the bottom end of your project. Proceed like that with your other wing.

11

Comb all small cords and also the protruding longer cords. Fix that gorgeous project made of cords with hairspray. Cut your wing into shape.

12

Having finished both sides, you can take your angel and fix it with hot glue in its middle-section. Cut to measure another cord which and fix to the top of the heart, so you can hang up your angel. You may also hang up your heart without using a cord.

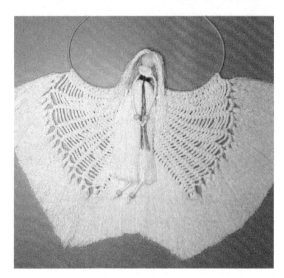

Chapter 17
Three-Dimensonal Tree

Since many years, the Christmas tree has been a decoration for our home during the festive season. Traditionally, it's a real tree. But who cares for the natural environment is looking for other options, too. This wonderful 3-D-Christmas tree could be one of these options. If you want to do without a real tree, the following instruction should be just the right for you.

Materials

- 3-D Metal tree
- Green Macrame yarn
- White Macrame yarn
- Light chain
- Pair of scissors

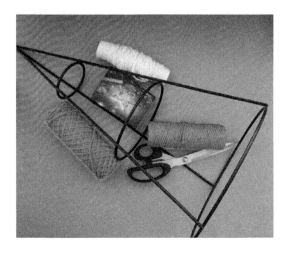

1

Cut off a long cord from the white yarn. Get a few drops of hot glue on the top of the tree and fix the end of the cord to it. Then you start off wrapping yarn around one of the three rods.

2

Having come to the small ring, you cut off the cord and fix it with hot glue. Then wrap yarn around the other two rods and proceed like before.

3

Wrap white yarn around the ring so that you can hide the glued spots of the cut-off cords. If your cord isn't long enough, you can insert a new cord by fixing it with hot glue.

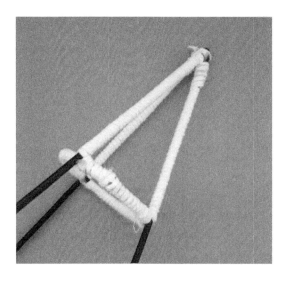

4

The snow-clad treetop is done. The rest of the tree is going to be green. For the straight rods, you cut to measure a cord with a length of about 200 cm. Double the cord and place it behind the rod. Then tie the cord in by means of a carrick bend. Place the cord on the left L-shaped over the rod. Take the cord on the right and place it over the L. Then move along its loose end under the rod and through the L-shaped loop. Pull both cords tight and do the same with the right side.

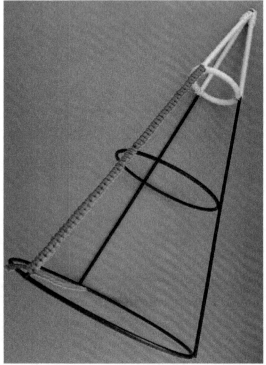

5

Then tie in the complete rod and fix the ends of the cords to the bottom part of the ring by using hot glue.

6

Wrap green yarn around both rings and fix the loose ends with glue, too.

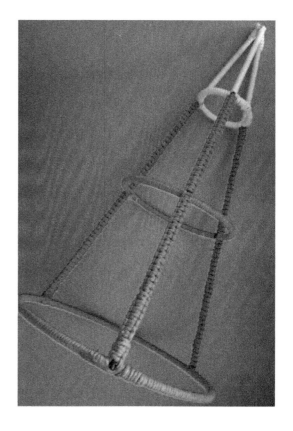

7

In order to turn on the lights of your tree, you may wrap the light chain around the tree. The switch should be positioned somewhere at the bottom of the tree.

8

Then, take yellow paper and cut out the shape of a star. Fix it to the top of your tree with some drops of glue. It's looking particularly pretty, if you place a light between two paper stars.

These instructions provide only a basic notion for your 3-D Macrame Christmas Star. How you decorate it, and which items you choose, is completely up to your creativity!

Chapter 18
Clipboard Or Macrame Board

Sometimes it's quite hard to create your Macrame projects properly as they haven't got the right stability. However, there are a few tricks you may think of to become a successful Macrame artist.

One option is to take adhesive tapes to fix your project to the table, or you choose a clipboard or a Macrame board.

But the most workable solution? What's the difference between a clipboard and a Macrame board?

The clipboard can be used to fix the top port of your Macrame project, so it can't slip in any way, and you can continue with your work. This clipboard is particularly suitable for less complicated projects like chains or wristbands. Should you work on a more complicated project like a coaster, it's going to be a bit more difficult.

For a coaster, for example, you better pick a board or a cork plate onto which you can pin your projects with needles and have the option to spin them, if necessary.

Using a proper board, you have an additional advantage: The edges are slightly indented, so you have the option to clamp your projects. The big advantage of a professional Macrame board, however, are the assist lines on it. They help you to tie your project straight.

However, there are projects that you neither fix to your table with adhesive tapes nor clamp to a clipboard or Macrame board. The reason being their size and the length of the yarn you need. For complex projects like curtains or carpets, it's best to tie them when being fixed to a clothes rail or any comparable bar like, for example, a wooden stick between two chairs. Particularly suitable are hooks that you can fix to chairs or doors. They can be used to hang up a stick or the project and start working.

Which option is the best for you, you have to find out yourself by simply testing them and making your experience with Macrame.

Knotting more complicated projects

As for more complicated projects, it's really better to use assisting means like a clothes rail. But there are other tricks as well which can be very helpful for finishing your big project successfully.

- ❖ **The proper measures:** You've got an idea that you want to put into practice? Or you have seen a Macrame project somewhere on the Net you'd like to copy? In that case, you should find out about the measures of the yarn you need. Ask for help, instructions and measures in Macrame Groups.

- ❖ **What to do with all the yarn?** When knotting more complicated and big projects, your cords will be much longer than for less complex projects. In order to prevent the cords from entangling, you can roll up the individual cords, gather them and make them into bundles. Use hooks or clamps to dispose of the cords you don't need for the time being. This way you always keep your project clearly structured.

- ❖ **Cardboard as wild card:** To keep the cords properly apart, you can cut to measure cardboard stripes with the measures you need. You can insert these stripes wherever you want, and you always know how far or how tight you have to tie your next knot.

- ❖ **Proper cutting:** You may use cardboard for this purpose as well. Cut to measure the cardboard and place it on your project to cut off neatly any protruding parts.

- ❖ **Avoid fraying:** In order to prevent the cord ends to become frayed, you can wrap adhesive tape around them. That's very recommendable, even for smaller projects.

- ❖ **Clips:** These tools can help you to put your longer cords into order and to roll them up.

- ❖ **Difficult knots:** Knots which are difficult for you to tie should be practiced with remaining yarn. Thus, you make sure that you know how to tie your real Macrame projects.

Chapter 19
Bonus Project:
Advent Calendar

The most beautiful thing for kids in the festive season is the advent calendar. But you don't have to buy a calendar. How about a calendar that you've created yourself from small Macrame sacks?

Materials

- Macrame yarn in the colours of your choice
- Wooden sticks
- Comb
- Pair of scissors
- Cork plate
- Needles

1

Cut to measure a total of 20 cords with a length of your choice. Then prepare another cord you use for attaching your other cords. That one should have the same length as your 20 working cords.

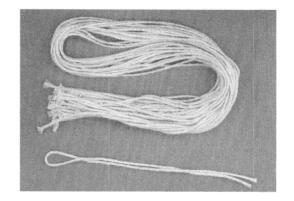

2

Double that latter cord and fix a small cord as your wild card in the middle. Take a few needles and fix the cord to the pinboard. Then wrap your 20 cords around the pinned cord with an anchor knot. Double the cord for this purpose, move the loop under the pinned cord and pull the loose ends through the loop, tightening the knot. Repeat these steps with your other cords until you've got ten cords fixed on each side.

3

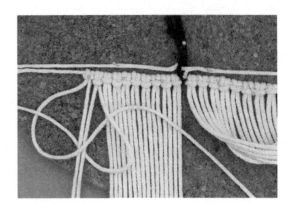

Start off with a side of your choice and make a row of carrick bends, for which purpose you need four cords next to each other. Place the left cord L-shaped over the two middle cords. Take the right cord, place it over the L-shaped cord and pull the loose end from the bottom through the L-loop. Repeat these steps with the other side, since a carrick bend is always made of two single knots.

4

After that, you put aside two cords on each side. Now, you tie another row of carrick bends, which is going to be offset. Take two cords from two carrick bends you've made already.

5

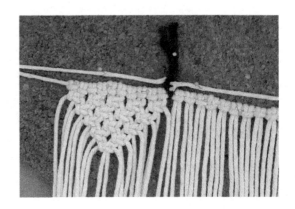

Do the same with the other rows of bends. Take two cords from each side and tie a row of offset carrick bends so that, finally, you obtain a triangle. Repeat the whole with the other side.

6

Now start to tie both triangles together, for which purpose you use a carrick bend. Make sure that the bends are in their respective row.

7

Having tied the triangles together, you can take your project from the pinboard and double it. Now, everything must be tied in the same way on the other side of your project. Make sure you do it exactly as before and that the new carrick bends remain in their respective rows.

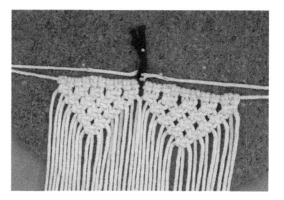

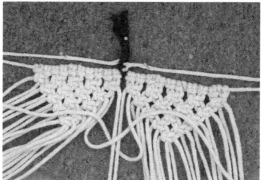

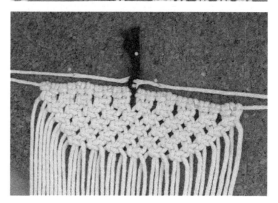

8

Having everything on the same level, I recommend putting your project over a bottle, which makes it easier for you to tie row-wise. Every once in a while, you may take down the sack to check its size.

9

When your rows have been finished, you take your sack from the bottle and stick it between your knees. What's following now is probably the most difficult part of your work. You have to close the bottom of your project.

10

Put aside two cords at the top end of the bottom part. You don't need them. Take a cord from the rows of bends that are opposite on both sides. Align them in such a manner as to make them into a knot. Proceed like that until all your cords are tied with each other. There will be two cords remaining at the bottom end, which you don't need. Important: Pull all knots as tight as possible, so nothing can get loose again,

11

You're about done! What remains to be done is cut to length the protruding yarn at the bottom. Cut them to measure and comb the ends well. Connect both loose ends at the top edge with a tight knot which is close to the edge of the sack.

12

Cut to measure four very long cords with a minimum length of 230 cm. Tie about 60 carrick bends in the middle and fix the first stick to the net of cords. Take the first cord on each side and wrap it around the rod one time as to create a loop under it. Pull the loose end through the loop. Repeat this step, so your cord can become stable. Do the same with the other three cords as well as with the four cords on the right side. Then decide how far they're supposed to be apart and fix the other sticks in the same way.

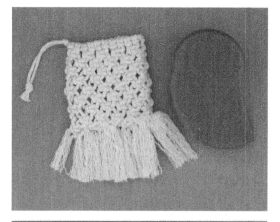

13

Fix all sacks to the sticks. It's up to you whether all of your 24 sacks are supposed to be tied Macrame-style or whether you wish to make further sacks from little pieces of cloth, as you can see in the image. You may use these cloth sacks for sweets or nice candies.

Closing Remarks

Macrame is a wonderful technique you can use to create enchanting items of decoration or presents. Apart from that, you can use Macrame to get away from your daily routine and find relaxation. Particularly, the festive season is very often experienced as stressful and exhausting.

With this book on Macrame, you will have the opportunity to make the festive season as cozy as you wish. Get started and create yourself a quiet and relaxing time to prepare in the best possible way for Christmas.

Should you still be looking for Christmas presents, you will surely be able to create this or that Macrame-style present. Imagine the bright shining eyes of all those people who will get these wonderful presents, of all those who will hold in their hands a Macrame angel that you made yourself.

But you might also like to decorate your home in a completely different Christmas-like manner. Perhaps you wish to surprise your child or your partner with a self-tied advent calendar. I'm sure this book will provide enough incentives and ideas for achieving that kind of joy.

Off you go with the knots! Tie yourself a relaxing Christmastime and enjoy the wonderful stillness that you can create for yourself by working on Macrame projects.

Did you enjoy this book?

Dear Readers,

Are you happy with this book? Is it meeting your expectations?
If yes, I'm looking forward to your comments, praise, criticism and ideas.

I would be pleased to receive your feedback on Amazon and give me the chance to improve.

Thank you in advance!

Cordially yours,

Vivien Romhoffer

Disclaimer

The implementation of all information, instructions and strategies contained in this book is at your own risk. The author cannot be held liable for any damages of any kind for any legal reason. Liability claims against the author for material or non-material damages caused by the use or non-use of the information or by the use of incorrect and/or incomplete information are excluded in principle. Therefore, any legal and damage claims are also excluded. This work was compiled and written down with the greatest care and to the best of our knowledge. However, the author accepts no re-sponsibility for the topicality, completeness and quality of the information. Printing errors and mis-information cannot be completely excluded. No legal responsibility or liability of any kind can be assumed for incorrect information provided by the author.

Copyright

Impressum

© Vivien Romhoffer
2023
1st edition
All rights reserved.
Reprinting, even in extracts, is not permitted.
No part of this work may be reproduced, duplicated or distributed in any form without the written permission of the author.
Contact us: Mark Lipke, Kuhanger 9, 31787 Hameln-Germany
Cover design: B.M.
Cover:Deposit

Printed in Great Britain
by Amazon

47966602R00071